Memoirs of A Girl Prophet

Memoirs of A Girl Prophet

Yaa Carson

Copyright © Yaa Carson 2023

ISBN: Softcover   978-1-941574-19-5
       E-Book   978-1-941574-20-1

All rights reserved. No part of this book may be reproduced or transmitted in any form or by any means, electronic or mechanical, including photocopying, recording, or by any information storage and retrieval system, without permission in writing from the copyright owner.

Unless otherwise indicated, all scriptural quotations are from The Holy Bible - King James Version.

Contents and/or cover may not be reproduced or transmitted in whole or in part in any form or by any means electronic or mechanical, including photocopying, recording, or by any information storage and retrieval system without the express written consent of the publisher.

This book was printed in the United States of America.

To order additional copies of this book, contact:
globalworldministries@yahoo.com

DEDICATION

To the Father, Son, and Holy Spirit …

I dedicate this book to the Trinity who governs the earth. You have guided me since I took my first breath. You have never forbidden me your love and kindness. I will forever cherish our relationship. Thank you for always being present.

ACKNOWLEDGEMENTS

To my mother, Linda Ann Wimbish Fussell, thanks mama for always encouraging me to be great in everything I do. I miss you dearly, but I know that you are watching over me from Heaven. To my big sister Kenyatta, thank you for the push to get this book finished and share with the world our story. I love you dearly.

To my children Marquis, Christopher, Indya, Zachariah and Anna, God gave me His best when He gave me you all. Thank you all for your love, admiration, and thoughtfulness. I am so proud that you all call me Mama.

To my dear sweet husband Marc, thank you for understanding me when I did not understand myself. Thank you for always being there and going beyond exhibiting true selflessness. I love you with the deepest love.

TABLE OF CONTENTS

Introduction	9
Chapter 1 – Mama, Who Is That in My Room	11
Chapter 2 - Vision of The Crown	21
Chapter 3 – A Mighty Rushing Wind Left Me	27
Chapter 4 – Give Me Your Hand	36
Chapter 5 - National and Global Impartation	41
Chapter 6 – Holy Spirit Sat on My Bed and Cried	51
Chapter 7 - A Consuming Fire	59
Chapter 8 – Vision Of 9/11	61
Chapter 9 – Arms of Vines Dream	65
Chapter 10 – Thorn in My Flesh	69
Chapter 11 – Vision of The Lake of Fire	74
Chapter 12 – The Coming of the Lord Dream	76
Information	81

WWW.
GlobalWorldMinistries.org

INTRODUCTION

This biography, *Memoirs of A Girl Prophet*, is a collection of notable supernatural and divine events that happen in the life of a young girl named Yaa Carson. The events are chronicled into adulthood. She never understood that there was a mysterious Higher Being at work in her life. Yaa would hide these powerful supernatural and divine visitations and visits to different realms from her family and friends. The fear of being labeled *crazy* would silence her and keep her from releasing the experiences that she witnessed during her life. From Heavens' Angels to demonic forces, she encountered each and learned how to distinguish between the two. God began teaching her how to respond when one of the Trinity was present with her. "Is it Jesus, Holy Spirit, or you God," she learned to ask when one was present or when distinguishing the voice she was hearing.

Growing up Yaa did not have anyone to hold her hand and explain the events that only she could see. There was no one that could succinctly tell her who she was in the Kingdom of God. All she knew was that God would show up privately; all while showing her the deep and enigmatic levels of the prophetic realm. Longing for answers, she submitted her will unto God and answers of her destiny began to unveil.

In this book you will not only be engaged in the stories, but you will learn that you are not alone in experiencing this phenomenal gift of the prophetic that

God has given you. You may have a young child that is prophetically gifted, or you may be an adult still searching for answers. You have questioned why you know or see things unlike those around. This book is your guide to understanding what you have already experienced with the supernatural.

Chapter 1

Mama, Who is That in My Room?

When I was four years old, I can remember being able to *see*. Not just seeing in the physical sense but in a spiritual sense as well. Many nights when sleeping I would be quickly awakened because of a strong presence in my room with me. I was never frightened by this presence because it was always calm, and my room became very warm when it entered. I did not know what or who this presence was. So, whenever this presence entered my room at night I would sit straight up and then I would call out to my mom whose room was straight across the hall.

I would say, "mama somebody is in my room." And she would come and look around and say no one is here go back to sleep. As she would walk out my bedroom, I would ask her, "momma can I keep my lamp on?" And she would say yes. This happened a lot of nights during my childhood. I can remember walking to the kitchen through the living room and I would see these tall people wearing all white robe like garments. If I had to describe them, they looked to be of Native American descent. They were male with long dark colored hair, with wide faces, and high cheek bones. They did not smile, nor did they talk; they just stood there and looked puzzled. There could be several standing in the living room as I walked by. At the time, I did not know who these individuals were, they never said anything to me, but I noticed that my mom never saw them. I would look at them and look at her and then look back at them. I would stand between these individuals and my mother, who had no interaction with each other. My mom never even knew they were there. So, I did not entertain it, I did not know how to tell her what I saw. It was normal for me to see them not knowing that they were angels from heaven.

> *The angel of the LORD encamps all around those who fear Him And delivers them.*
> *Psalm 34:7*

While living in that same home on Rosewood Road in Atlanta, my older 6-year-old sister Kenyatta, would find these big, long white fluffy beautiful feathers, about the size of a man's hand in the hallway. I can remember hearing her say, "Mama look at what I found in the hallway!" She would shout holding the feather up so that Mama could see. Me, not remembering what Mama said back to her, had no clue of what the significance of a feather being in the house meant. But Kenyatta did and she would put them in a little white bible for kids that she kept tucked away somewhere in her bedroom. She saved the feathers for show and tell at school, but the day she went back to get the feathers from the bible they were gone! So, my question today is, who came to get their feathers? And why could she not keep them? And as the years went on and we grew older she never saw them again.

On several occasions I would sleep in my sisters' room and would still be visited by Heavenly beings. I can remember when I was in the fourth grade, we moved into a two-bedroom townhouse on Bouldercrest Road, and I was visited by two beings, a male, and a female. I sat up in my bed still sleepy but woke when a strong presence commanded my attention. I turned my head to the left toward the doorway and saw these two beings standing there looking directly at me.

Startled but not afraid, I whispered to my sister, "Kenyatta do you see them people in the room?"

She answered, "Nawl, I DO NOT see them people in the room. BUT I can feel them in here! NOW SHUT UP AND GO TO SLEEP!!" And just like that, Kenyatta threw the covers over her head to feebly block out their presence or movement. The two beings did not do anything but stand there and watch the room and as they watched us, I watched them back just to see if they were going to do anything. But they did not. I felt no threat, so I laid back down and went back to sleep because we had school the next day.

There is an unseen world around us that is extremely active. God has allowed some human beings the ability to see into that world sparingly. I am one of those people. But strangely all through my childhood, teenage years, and some of my adulthood I never ever told a soul. Mainly because of the fear of what people would think. I still struggle with that at times. But to this day if no one else ever believes me when I say that I see something from or in another realm, Kenyatta does. Because she was the one that had to endure those nightly visitations from beings from other realms. God always has a witness around whenever He does anything on earth and my big sister is my very own personal witness of the works of God in my life. God, our Father, is masterful in everything that He does and everything that He does has a specific purpose. It is up to us to search and discover what His plans are for our lives.

Growing up I always felt safe as though I knew someone was with me; as odd as it sounds, I still feel that way today. No matter where I may go in the world, I still feel those same angels present with me. At twenty-six years old I got married and moved from my hometown Atlanta, and relocated with my husband to Lexington, North Carolina. Late one night my husband and I were asleep, and I was awakened by the same pleasant presence and warmth that was in my bedroom as a child. But this time I saw his face closeup! And yes, I was startled because this Angel was an angel of war. His hair was bright gold, and his face was the widest face I had ever seen. Oddly he was not looking at me; although I could have reached out and touched his face with him being so close. He was actually looking in the direction of my bedroom door. So, I peeled back the covers from my face so that I could get a closer look at what was happening in my bedroom. When I turned, I saw one of his wings had stretched out over our king-sized bed and covered my husband and I. He was asleep and I could not believe what I was seeing. Upon looking in the same direction, standing at my bedroom door was a dark being looking eye to eye with the angel guarding us. It was like this particular angel was not only protecting us from this dark being, but he was also assigned by God and ready to go to battle on our behalf.

I did not really know why the dark being was there, but God knew ahead of time and sent us protection as we slept! And if you are anything like me you must know that I was a bit nosey about what was happening. However, I was not fearless enough to intervene in the middle of a battle in a different realm. Only the Father has the authority to intervene between spiritual and natural battles.

> *For He will command His angels concerning*
> *you to guard you in all your ways.*
> *Psalm 91:11*

So, content, I then snuggled closer to my husband, got under his arm, and pulled the covers back over me and went to sleep.

I saw the same angel again on a different occasion but this time I saw his eyes and his eyes were a piercing fiery blue—piercing through my soul. It felt like he was recording my thoughts and then he went up and I did not see him anymore. On a different occasion I saw the same angel in midair between the heavens and the earth. He was looking down directly at me as though God had sent him to check in on me. Could this have been my very own personal angel? We had a lot of angelic visitations in that house in Lexington.

Earth is an extremely spiritual world. God has allowed some of us the ability to see and hear in another realm. Some peoples' discerning gifts are stronger than others, some people may see or hear in the supernatural only once in a lifetime and others see and hear their entire lifetime. These are called seers. Sometimes they may be preachers or pastors but their assignment and purpose is to see, hear, and record for the next generation.

Memoirs of a Girl Prophet

1 I will stand at my watch and station myself on the ramparts; I will look to see what he will say to me, and what answer I am to give to this complaint. 2 Then the Lord replied: "Write down the revelation and make it plain on tablets so that a herald may run with it. 3 For the revelation awaits an appointed time; it speaks of the end and will not prove false. Though it linger, wait for it; it will certainly come and will not delay.
Habakkuk 2

    We have always known that curses can be passed down to the third and fourth generations of those who do not honor the Lord. However, spiritual gifts also can. When I realized that Marquis, my eldest son, could see in different realms he was about seven years old. Marquis was the type of kid that was always mature and wise beyond his years and remains that way today.

    I can remember one morning we were getting ready for our day, and he said something that stopped Marc and I in our tracks. Marquis said, "I saw an angel standing in y'all's bedroom door last night," just calmly, and nonchalantly, like normal.

    Marc and I both looked at each other and simultaneously said, "What?"

    Marquis went on saying, "Yeah, I got up in the middle of the night to go pee and I saw an angel standing at y'all's door looking at y'all."

    Marc asked, "What was the angel doing?"

    Marquis quipped, "Nothing just looking at y'all sleeping."

    "What did the angel look like?" I asked.

Marquis looked thoughtful and said, "He had on white with something gold wrapped around him and had something gold in his hand."

Marc being practical said, "Well did you go to the bathroom?"

Sheepishly Marquis said, "No I was scared and went back to bed and held it." We all burst out laughing and went about our day.

Angels are very real and at work in this realm today, just as they were in the days of Mary and Joseph in the Bible. Every person on this earth has assigned angels from God the Father. I learned that God assigns to every child that is born a legion of angels during their lifetime.

> *Do you think I cannot call on my Father, and he will at once put at my disposal more than twelve legions of angels?*
> *Matthew 26:53*

Just think, God has a certain number of angels assigned to your life to guard over you, to fight for you, to guide you, to speak to you, to record your thoughts, to wipe and catch your tears in bowls, to work healings through God for you, and just be a part of your everyday life. Supernatural experiences are happening everyday around the world and angels play a huge part in that.

Angels have a legal right to operate in the natural realm as well as the supernatural realm. We as people have the authority to speak into the supernatural on our behalf or on the behalf of someone else through the Words of God. So, when we try or operate in any other capacity it is called witchcraft. And that is illegal in the eyes of our Lord. He never meant for His power to be misused or misunderstood. But that is for another chapter.

Can you imagine casually walking in the hallway and instantaneously notice angels sitting all around, dressed in heavenly gold army attire? Yes, I saw that, and it almost scared me to death. It was an open vision that came to me like a flash of bright light. Angels were literally everywhere in the house, sitting comfortably in every corner. Not on guard but relaxed as though they had been there for a while.

Angels can also come to you in a natural form. When I was pregnant with my second child Chris, I can remember in 1993, a man knocked at my front door one day. I ran downstairs to answer the door but I always, ALWAYS, peeped through the curtain to see who was at the door before opening it. The door was partially glass so that is why the curtain was necessary. At the door was an older black man with a beard, wearing casual clothes. Nothing out of the norm, just a man.

I saw no threat, so I opened the door and said, "Hello?"
"Hello, did you know that children were God's gift to the world?" He said matter-of-factly.
Without thinking, I said, "Yes, I know."
"Well, I just was in the neighborhood and wanted to tell you that. Have a good day now," and off he trotted.
Nonchalantly I shrugged my shoulders and said, "Ok."

I closed the door and ran back upstairs to look out the window to see what house this man went to next. But I did not see him. So, I ran back downstairs to open the door to get a good look. And just like that, the man was gone; he had vanished. I thought I was crazy until the words came to me; *you just entertained an Angel.* Standing on the front porch still looking around my jaw dropped. I was stunned. After that, questions began to flood my mind. *Why did he tell me that? Why did God send him to me? How did he know I was pregnant because I was not showing? And why was I even able to witness this?* I will never ever forget that day nor forget the feeling of how special or important that the baby I was carrying must be to God. Because we, all of His children, are the apple of His eye.

> *Keep me as the apple of the eye; Hide me in the shadow of Your wings Psalm 17:8*

> *For thus says the Lord of hosts, After glory He has sent me against the nations which plunder you, for he who touches you, touches the apple of His eye. Zechariah 2:8*

The child in my womb was just two months old, but God sent an angel to me about him. So, I named him Christopher Angel because an angel came to us in plain clothes. And yes, Chris is definitely an anointed person highly favored of the Lord and also has a high sensitivity of the presence of God when He is near. God cares so much for us and actually wants us to simply acknowledge His existence. All we have to do is slow down, stop, and pay attention to His presence on this earth. And to be honest, all He really wants from us is to have a personal relationship with Him.

Chapter 2

Vision of the Crown

As usual, I was sitting on the side of my bed as if I were waiting for someone. Not really thinking about anything because my mind was incredibly quiet. I have learned that about myself, when God is about to speak to me or show me something I suddenly get very still and quiet. Not as though I am in a trance, because I'm fully aware of my surroundings, but similar. Before I knew it, I was in the third heaven sitting at the longest dinner table I had ever seen in my life. The table stretched for miles; so far that I could not see the beginning or the end. It was decorated with the finest of white linen tablecloths, the purest golden dinnerware and golden cutlery with intricate details. There were many crystal wine glasses and other grand décor. The splendor of it all was unmatchable and incomparable to anything on earth. I remember that warmth of the room felt like the same soft warmth that I would feel in my bedroom as a child. Immediately I knew that I was sitting at the Lords table in heaven. There I saw many people that served the Lord on earth. I will not give the names of the people but many of you would know them if I called them out. And since I did not get their permission to mention their names, I will not say them. But some of the people of God were great servants and have brought many to Christ.

Everyone seated at the table seemed confident that they were supposed to be sitting at the enormously long table. I looked up and saw these gigantic translucent male hands. The hands were huge, like when an adult sized hand enters a dollhouse to set up the miniature furnishings. The hands had a bright glow, and they were so big that they completely covered the top of the ceiling. These hands began placing golden crowns on the heads of the people at the table. The golden crowns were of all different shapes and sizes and had bright precious stones in them. In order, God Himself went down the line on one side of the table. Finally, it was my turn to receive my crown; so, I lowered my head down a little so that the Father could place my crown perfectly on my head. But in a flash, I was transported out of the room, away from that beautiful table and I looked around and darkness was all around me. No, I was not in hell or anywhere close to it but somewhere in the heavens—in a different dimension where the only light that shown was the light from God Himself.

As I knelt on my knees with my head lowered, I heard a loving voice as wide and deep as the ocean, saying, "Yaa you cannot enter in like that,"–he paused– "You have jealousy in your heart." Wait... what? Not me, I had no clue that jealousy was hidden in my heart. And just then my mind went to something that I had been longing for and I saw someone that I knew with it. I did not realize that such a small secret desire took hold in my heart so that jealousy slipped in. I cannot describe the overwhelming great sorrow and embarrassment that I had kneeling before the Father in that moment. I immediately apologized to the Father and before I could blink, in a flash I was transported back in my seat at the table, and with humility I lowered my head and received my crown. (Which is why crowns are so special to me because I saw my heavenly crown). It amazes me how quick God can forgive and forget within a twinkling of an eye. Then reward you as if sin were never there.

The definition of sin is a word, deed, or desire in opposition to the eternal law of God. (Referenced According to Augustine of Hippo)

> *26 that He might sanctify and cleanse her with the washing of water by the word, 27that He might present her to Himself a glorious church, not having spot or wrinkle or any such thing, but that she should be holy and without blemish. Ephesians 5*

You see we, the Saints of God, will not enter into the Kingdom of God and stay in His presence in the new world with any minute sin hidden in our hearts. It is impossible to live with God in His heavenly kingdom with a defiled heart. IMPOSSIBLE. Scriptures teach us how the high priest would have bells on the hem of their robes before they entered into the Holy of Holies. So that if the bells stopped ringing someone from outside would know that they died. Think about that for a moment. God's presence is so pure that you will die before Him because of sin in the heart. Absolutely nothing defiled can stand in the presence of Him and survive. Not even an evil desire in the heart that has not been performed as a physical act. Because of the darkness in my heart, the Father chastised me and removed me from inside of His kingdom momentarily until I fully repented of what was in my heart upon which I had not acted. Father did not give it time to manifest! You see, He loves us so much that He will come to us and tell us about ourselves first;

so that we, the church, will repent from our fleshly desires before we act them out in the natural.

Delivered from Rebellion

I remember a time years after this encounter with Father, I was in a deep sleep. Father woke me up, I sat up on my bed and quickly swung my feet to the floor. I began to feel Holy Spirit in the room with me, standing very close. How did I know He was there; you may wonder. Because I felt His love for me in that moment. And in a flash, I felt something leave my body, I looked up and saw a small vapor that quickly disappeared in the air.

Knowing that Holy Spirit was in the room, I calmly and humbly whispered to Him, "What was that?"
He answered lovingly, "I just delivered you from rebellion."

I did not ask how it got there; I did not even know it was there. I was just glad it was gone and that I was so on the Heart of God that He continues to show *me love*. But in the back of my mind, I was thinking, "But Lord, I serve you how could this be in me? I do not outwardly sin, I do not smoke or drink strong drink, my goodness I do not even cuss anymore. I try to be kind to everyone I meet. I do not backbite about folks; you speak to me to directly and I can hear you. I'm friendly to everyone so how could things be in my heart that I'm not aware of?" It is this simple.

Behold, I was shaped in iniquity; and in sin did my mother conceive me. Psalm 51:5

We all come in the earth with something. You may have the same as me or something totally different. But we all come in the world with something. That is why it is important for us not to pass judgment on others just because we do not familiarize ourselves with their battles. And as we walk out this thing called life; we must continue to stay in the face of God so that He continues to wash our hearts clean. So that in the day of the coming of the Lord we will be blameless in His sight. On several occasions, the Lord has shown me glimpses of rooms inside of the kingdom of Heaven. And always everywhere was surrounded by the brightest and purest light with the same warmth I felt in my bedroom as a little girl. The citizens that lived there were always calm and peaceful, yet busy at work tending to their assignments.

I call them citizens because not all of them were angels. In Heaven, the moment that you arrive you have an immediate knowing of who everyone is. You will even know the animals by name as though they were your very own pets. (I have experienced this in a similitude.) Remarkably they all will know who you are as well. In His kingdom we really are one body, one family. I used to have trouble understanding why God called the church His bride but after many occasions of seeing things from His view I get it now. He simply calls the church His bride because of how He wants to continually adorn us with the very best His kingdom has to offer. And just as a bride on earth prepares herself with the finest of jewelry, gowns and perfumes for her big day, our Father wishes to do the same for us for eternity. We are the apple of His eye remember. Out of all the creatures He has ever made in this world, worlds before us, and worlds to come, we the church—His bride, are the only beings that our Lord created that He calls the apple of His eye.

Chapter 3

A Mighty Rushing Wind Left Me

A huge turning point in my life was 1996. I was 22 years old. Atlanta had the Olympics going on and the city was booming with growth, innovative ideas, new people etc. It was an extremely wonderful time to live in Atlanta. I was versatile and was modeling, styling hair, traveling, and meeting all kinds of people in the entertainment world. Some people I still cannot believe that I had the opportunity to meet in person. And of course I was trying everything under the sun that I could do that I could easily get away with (but I still had a conscious). That is what you are supposed to do when you are in your early twenties, be young and carefree, right?

But there was still this strong tug from God Himself on me. So even when I would smoke a little weed or try to cuss folks out when they made me angry, I could look up at the sky and the clouds would be in formation looking like Peter, James and John, and the Apostles, looking back at me. And I would immediately lose my high and straighten up as if my mother was in the room. Even in those moments I knew that one day I would surrender my all to God, but I just was not ready to do it at that time. I wanted what I wanted, and I did not want all of God in those days. I only wanted His protection to cover me from all of my foolishness, and He did. And those that really knew me well, knew that I was on my way to Hollywood. Acting, singing—I took my shot at it all. I just knew that I was on my way to Hollywood. Which was a promise I made to my Mom when I was five. However, God had other plans for my life of which I was aware.

I was working at a salon on the east side of Atlanta alongside my best friend Tracie Edmonds Who by the way is another person besides my sister that has always told me, "Yaa you do not lie so if you ever was to tell me that you saw a green man under the bed, I will believe you." It is funny how I did not recognize destiny at that time but found out years later that even in my years of folly I was right on course.

I was working at the salon one Friday afternoon when a woman with the kindest eyes came into the salon to get her hair done. I cannot remember who her stylist was that day, but she was a regular every week. The sister was short with silver gray hair and walked with authority. She was the kind of lady that if you did not know her you would figure out a way to make you're her acquaintance. We called her Rev. Sherrie. Rev. Sherrie held weekly meetings at a local woman and children's shelter on the southwest side of Atlanta. Oddly, I cannot remember how I got involved with going to these meetings, but I can remember who went. Sabrina and Nikki, both co-stylists at the salon, and I. We all would sometimes go to the Women's shelter to listen to the messages that Rev. Sherrie would preach. Then somehow, we would end up at Rev. Sherrie's home discussing the Holy Spirit.

Holy Spirit, A name that I often heard from my then pastor, Bishop Earl Paulk, growing up at church. A name that I often heard my mother called God many times. A name that I would be drawn to as I got to know more of his character. Even though I was not paying attention to His name at church or when my mom spoke of Him. But tiny seeds were dropping in my heart as I heard them speak His name. And yes, I would say that I knew the name before I understood who He is.

One evening while at Rev. Sherrie's, Sabrina found a book on the living room table. She picked it up and said, "Rev. Sherrie what's this book about?"
Rev. Sherrie answered, "That is a book about the Holy Spirit, He's a gentleman you know."

I made my way over to see what the book looked like. And to my surprise I immediately recognized the book because I had seen the exact book on my mother's bed or on her dresser or her bookshelf. I had seen that book all around my house laying wherever my mom was reading it at the time. For whatever reason I was never drawn to even pick it up.

So, I said, "Oh my mother has that book at home."
Rev. Sherrie said, "She does, have you ever read it?"
Me, "No."
Rev. Sherrie: "You ought to read it, it teaches you who the Holy Spirit is."

Her tone in speaking of the Holy Spirit made my interest grow in reading the book. I had to learn of this person that she spoke so highly about. So, when I got home, I searched the house for the highly recommended book. I went into my mother's bedroom and there it was just as it had been for several years. *Good Morning Holy Spirit,* by Benny Hinn.

I reached down picked it up and turned to my mom, who was sitting on the side of her bed looking at me and said, "Mama can I read this book?"

And she simply said "Yes," with a slight smile on her face. As though she already knew that my perception of who I thought God is would change to a deeper level.

It did just that. I finally found the one who had entered my bedroom as a child. While reading that book Holy Spirit would visit me at times and I became to know Him as a person. Only because He came to me. Words were not spoken we just sat in quietness and watched as though He was waiting on me to **say** something and I was waiting on Him to **do** something. I knew His presence when it would fill my room. It was that same warm bright light that illuminated my bedroom on Rosewood Road when I was a little girl. Even though His presence was startling, I was not afraid. His presence always brought me peace and I would fall asleep as He left. No one can ever tell me that God is not real. *He comes to those that He chooses. I did not ask Him to, nor did I know to ask, He just came.*

One Sunday morning worship service at the Women's shelter. Rev. Sherrie asked if we wanted to go on a Women's Retreat. So, Sabrina, Nikki, and I all said yes. We prepared ourselves for this journey that would change our lives forever. We arrived at the retreat not really knowing what was about to take place. We all knew that we wanted to receive the Holy Spirit in our hearts as Rev. Sherrie had taught us. At the end of one of the night services at the retreat, Rev. Sherrie asked if anyone wanted to receive the Holy Spirit. And we looked at each other and nervously we all said, "yes."

So, we got up from our seats, along with other young women who had come to the retreat and slowly walked to the front of the room. Rev. Sherrie stood there waiting to pray for us. One by one, she prayed for us to receive the Holy Spirit. There was not any shouting, dancing around the room, hollering, tarrying, and no one was falling out on the floor. Just a sweet gentle touch from Rev. Sherrie's small warm hand on the top of my head and I immediately felt my stomach rolling with a power I did not understand. Tears softly rolled down my cheeks, my mouth began to open, and out of my mouth words that I could not comprehend forcibly rolled off my tongue without my control. Then I heard Rev. Sherrie whisper in my ear, "Rivers of Living Water shall come from you."

Whoever believes in Me, as the Scriptures said, 'Out of his belly shall flow rivers of living water. John 7:38

No, I did not completely understand what was happening to me in that moment but did not resist it. However, it became clear that it would be a part of me forever. As we went back to our hotel room tears still strolling down my face, I was still speaking the unknown language uncontrollably.

I remember turning to Sabrina and saying, "I cannot stop, it will not stop."

And when she said, "I cannot either," as tears streamed down her face, I stopped feeling strange because then I knew what was happening to me, was happening to her and Nikki too.

During this time, I was dating a man fifteen years older than me, that I allowed to take control over a lot of my thinking and even some of my decision making. Even though I was on a journey to find my oneness in God I was still entangled with worldly desires. Meaning my flesh was still untamed if you know what mean. I had given God my heart, but I have not yet given Him my life. After receiving this gift of the Holy Spirit, I knew very well that He was alive living on the inside of me.

And I understood by my reading of the Bible that my body was cleansed from all previous sins. But as I mentioned before I still had worldly fleshly desires and habits that needed to be put under subjection. That part takes time and significant effort. I was in a wonderful place in my life with this new understanding of who Holy Spirit was. Finally, I was developing a love affair with this presence that would come and visit me from time to time. Such a love affair it was! Such inner peace I began to have. But I still had to deal with the desires that would come up at times. I was facing decisions to stay holy, and acceptable unto God, pleasing Him only or pleasing myself with worldly fantasies and pleasures only for a moment.

While dating this older man I began to realize that he had a lot of influence over my thoughts and decisions. His thoughts ruled the relationship because my thoughts were not yet strong enough in knowing who I was or what I genuinely wanted out of life. So, I put more value in his thoughts because he had two businesses, a production company had been married and divorced, drove a Porsche, lived in Buckhead Atlanta, been to prison and lived to talk about it all. Yes, the guy lived a pretty interesting life that caught my attention, and he also bought me my 1st Chanel bag, so I was in! I was in my early twenties remember, so he knew what could lure a young lady. But what I was about to experience in that relationship taught me how to value what truly matters in life. Being in that relationship taught me today how to protect the anointing that God gives us—after receiving the Holy Spirit in my life and building a relationship with God the Father.

I decided to abstain from sex or anything unholy. So, I kind of broke off that relationship because I knew that staying in it did not include God. And I said 'kind of broke off' because I was not done with him yet. We would still go out for dates and of course he would try to pull me back in a relationship. He was extremely persistent, so I let my guard down and let him back in. So, one night as we sat and talked, watched a couple of movies, and ate a nice dinner, I found myself in his bed again, but this was for sure the last time. The Bible teaches that God is holy and Holy Spirit will not dwell in an unclean temple. He is a gentleman and wants to be recognized as such, He is easily grieved when we are not sensitive to the unction of His presence.

> *For if any man defile the temple of God, God will destroy him. For the temple of God is holy and that is what you are. 1 Corinthians :17 Therefore, brothers, by the mercies of God, I urge you to present your bodies as a living sacrifice, holy and pleasing to God; this is your spiritual worship. Romans 12:1*

So, we as God's children, must keep our bodies as a living sacrifice unto Him.

My dear friends, that is exactly what I did not do, present my body as a living sacrifice unto God. But in my defense I did not know how to it. So, after we finished, I got up to go and shower like I normally would. But as I walked from the bed into the hallway I felt this strong rushing wind leave my body.

And I whispered to myself, "WHAT WAS THAT?!"

And I heard Holy Spirit audibly say, "I just left your body." And just like that He was gone.

So, I began to think, "maybe a window was open and the wind came through that is why I felt the wind." So, I checked the windows, and they were all closed. And then it hit me, I no longer had the fight in me to stand against temptation when it came.

After that day I was back at square one with having to try to avoid temptation but sadly I would give in every time. See friends, what I did was sin against my own body by not keeping my covenant with God the Father so His spirit, the gentleman, left my body.

> *Flee from fornication. Every sin that a man does is outside the body; but he that commits fornication sins against his own body. 1 Corinthians 6:18*

And even though I could still speak in my heavenly language, feel His presence and could at times hear His voice, He was not living in me as He once did. In fact, He did not take any of His gifts from me that I could use in the kingdom, He simply took back His Spirit.

Hear me when I say this, sometimes when you see ministers fornicating or doing unholy acts in the church and still preaching every Sunday without remorse, it is because the Father recognizes that this is a man or woman that knows Him. So, He will leave grace to cover them as they do the work for the kingdom. God recognizes that laborers are few in number, so He has to use who is a willing vessel for His Glory. Whether we agree with it or not. The work has to get done before Christ returns!

Tears well up in my eyes as I write this because I remember the pain and agony of knowing that I had failed Him once again. I had begged for Holy Spirit to come back to dwell in me again, but it was not until I turned twenty-six and was pregnant with my daughter Indya that He decided to come back and live inside me again. And when He came back, God also touched my womb and Indya spoke in tongues in my womb. And then I regained the power to be able to stand and fight against any temptation that came my way. Grace stepped in for me once again. It was because of His grace for me that He decided to come back. I fully understand that now, so I protect the anointing and I honor the relationship that we have, not allowing the interference of fleshy desires to break relationship between God and I. God Himself came to me first; so, then I was on a quest like the Apostle Paul to find out who it was that apprehended me.

Chapter 4

Give me your hand!

God has always made sure to make His presence known to me in my life. Even during those times I did not want to acknowledge Him being there. It did not matter to Him that He would still have to give me small signals to adore Him. God loves an audience, and He is extremely detailed about everything that He does on earth, as well as in heaven. I have never been the type to put too much thought into religion, whether I would find myself engrossed in God Himself. Probably because of the fact that He introduced Himself to me very early in life. So, my thoughts of church or its traditions in religion do not move me whatsoever. I have often wondered why I do not like to go to church. Is there something wrong with me? Because I absolutely love God the Father with all my heart. So, what is the disconnection that I have for entering the church itself?

The answer is simple. My love affair started the day He entered into my bedroom as a little girl so whenever I go inside of a church and do not feel that same love from His presence, I am quickly bored with formalities and traditions. I have made His personality my "church," therefore, my life became His church. In fact, I applaud some of the acts that I see happening in today's church. And in my quiet time with Him I will ask how He feels about what is happening in church today. Sometimes He will answer me, and His mood is always sad when talking about the church. I will go into more in detail in another chapter. Nevertheless, I have learned to take the good and leave the bad of it all.

As my love for God the Father grew, I can remember a day during my courtship with Marc, when I was visiting his high-rise apartment in Midtown Atlanta. At the time Marc worked a night shift job and went to school during the day. His apartment was a one bedroom on the third floor. There were large ceiling to floor windows that I used to love to sit by and stare down at the diverse communities of people walking and driving about on Piedmont Rd. I would see the most interesting people walking by, and I would hear all the sounds of the busy city. Ambulances or police sirens would always be heard well into the middle of the night. But on one particular night as he was preparing to leave, he looked at me and said, "Make sure you lock the front and back door." And I did as he instructed which was not out of the norm. He has a protective nature, so he wanted me to be safe.

As usual I followed him to the front door, kissed him goodbye, and closed it. Because he lived in the city you can bet that he had about three locks and a chain lock on the door. So, I made sure that I locked them all. Then I walked through the living room to the kitchen to lock the back door. Now because of that building being built in the 1940's the back door in the galley kitchen was actually an old fire escape. Which was directly across from his neighbors back door with stairs all the tenants in the building had access to. And the back door had one lock with a chain lock as well. I locked them all. Again, I locked them all.

I watched some TV in the cozy living room before going to bed around 10pm. Marc loves reading the Bible, so he had different versions of bibles laying around. These were the days before Bible apps. I began reading the Message Bible—I cannot remember the scriptures, but I loved the way the message Bible read. Drifting off to sleep with the Bible still in my hand the phone rang, it was Marc checking in on me while on his break. I had the TV in the living room still on, but the volume was turned all the way down because I did not want to hear any sound as I slept. But I needed the light from TV if I got up to use the bathroom. After hanging up the phone I reached over to turn off the lamp next to the bed. Again, nothing unusual so I drifted off into a deep sleep. It is funny as you sleep you can still hear, feel, smell and have use of all five senses. Still with my eyes closed I remember the room getting warm and a bright light came on as if someone came in and flipped the light switch on. My eyes still closed when I heard these words, "Give me your hand." So, I reached out my hand and touched male fingers. I did not think anything about it because I thought it was Marc.

Morning came and I was awakened by the phone ringing, it was Marc calling to say he was on the way home. Wait a minute. "Did he not come home already?" I thought. I jumped out of the bed ran to the front door, looked and the chain was still engaged. So, being a little spooked I ran to the back door to check if it was opened but it was locked with the chain still in place—exactly as I left it. And then I heard the same voice that said, "Give me your hand," followed by, "It was Me." As if He was still in the house with me.

In the that moment I knew it was Jesus Yeshua whose hand that I touched. I fell to my knees and cried. Can you imagine the thoughts and questions running through my mind? To gather my thoughts, I sat down on the sofa and waited anxiously for Marc to come home. But the main question in my head was, *"Why in the world did He come to me? What does He want with me?"*

It seemed to take forever for him to get home that morning. When Marc finally came home, I asked him, "Did you come home last night?"
He said, "No, why?" Everything else was a blur after that.

Jesus, Yeshua just visited me. Thinking back on that night the love that I felt in the hand that I touched is like no other love I have ever felt. The warmth in the room was the exact same warmth I would feel in my room as a child. I then knew that God wanted me for something. For what, I did not know but for something! When God the Father sends an Angel, Jesus Yeshua, or Holy Spirit to show up to you directly there is an assignment on your life. Never take His visitation lightly; He will never overstep His will in your life. You must willingly yield your will to Him and then He will give you instructions for the assignment or purpose here on earth. As you stay on the path that God has mapped out for you, you will remain in His hands, covered, and protected by His grace, His love, and His blood. Even when you are faced with the hardest of trials, He is still with you. Even when you doubt Him, He is still there. It is only when you move away from His Will for your life that unnecessary troubles will affect you.

Chapter 5

National and Global Impartation

On August 5, 2008, the Lord woke me up saying these words, *National Impartation*. As He began to talk, I began wrestling with my flesh because it wanted to sleep but He wanted my ear. (Most people that walk in the prophetic deal with this battle of the will while sleepy.) As I began battling to fully wake up, I could hear Him tell me things concerning my future. He even gave me a scripture to read, Romans 10:12.

I read it and dozed right back off again. And that is when I heard Him say, "Anything that the flesh desires, I desire the opposite." That was all He had to say.

I quickly sat straight up in my bed ready to devour what He was going to say next. Now focused I asked Him, "What about National Impartation?"

He answered, "I am giving you a National Impartation, you are not ready for Global Impartation yet." I began questioning God about what all of this meant then He explained, "You are now ready to fight in the spirit on a national level but not yet on a global level." I pondered about writing that part down and He said, "Write that down." I smiled and obeyed. And then I began to feel my spirit man soar, but my body was still fixed in one place.

So, I questioned Him. "What is happening to me? Why can I feel my spirit soaring with you, but my body is still?" I also said, "How can my physical body catch up with my spiritual body?"

He simply said, "This is not your battle this is your husbands battle, pray him through it and then you will be released." Released to do what, I thought.

During this time Marc was about to be ordained as pastor of the church. He was going through some of the toughest battles of his life spiritually, with family members, his job, financially, and so forth. The battles just kept coming during this time of our lives. So being the wife that I am, I took on his battles as though I could fight them for him. It seemed that the more I tried to intervene the harder the battles became to overcome. It was not until an encounter with a national warlock, who physically entered our bedroom that we fought and won, that we found victory in the natural battles. Let me go deeper to bring you clarity.

For the weapons of our warfare are not carnal, but mighty through God to the pulling down of strongholds. 2 Corinthians 10:4

In the prophetic realm every upward level in God there must come a battle from the demonic realm. One evening as Marc and I were just drifting off to sleep I heard the Lord say, "For the next three nights you will be visited by a national warlock." I tapped Marc on his shoulder and repeated what I heard. We both thought nothing of it and went to sleep. The next day went on as normal, Marc went to work, and the kids went to school. I was eight months pregnant with Anna at the time, so I stayed home; only leaving the house to pick up the kids from school. But that night something happened that I will never forget. As the house got quiet, Marc and I drifted off to sleep. The next thing I knew was I was awakened because I heard something moving in the hallway in front of my bedroom doorway. The hall was dark so I could not see it very well. I sat up in bed to look harder, only to see this dark five foot being standing in my doorway looking at me and Marc laying in the bed. At that point, Marc was still sound asleep. So, I tapped him on his shoulder to see if he could see what I was seeing in the natural.

Marc turned and saw me staring at the doorway and said, "Honey what is it?" By this time Marc was used to me being able to see things in supernatural realms.

"Honey can you see that being standing at the doorway?

Marc said, "I cannot see it, but I know something is there I can feel it there, honey what is it, what do you see?

I said without hesitation, "I can see him Honey"—my heart was racing—"he has long dirty locks, old drapery clothes with a hood over his head, long black claw like fingernails, and clubbed like feet. But I cannot see his face. I cannot see his eyes it is like he does not have any."

This creature from hell started walking towards the bed and Marc must have felt it coming towards us because he jumped out the bed and hit the floor with the loudest travail that I had ever heard a man utter. Hesitantly, I began to travail as well; still looking at this thing that was looking at us. We both travailed with urgency until the sun came up. But I noticed that our travailing only made the warlock stand still, he quietly stood in the corner and did not leave until daybreak.

The next morning came and went, everything was back to its regular schedule. Then night came and the kids ate dinner, bathed, and went off to their beds. As Marc and I are having pillow talk, we looked at each other and remembered the night before. Then Marc said, "Did not the Lord say we would be visited for three nights?"
I said, "Yep." Silly of us to believe something different other than what God pre-warned us about, we watched a movie and went to sleep. Then we were awakened a second night to this same ugly thing that had to have permission by God the Father to try us. Again, he made his presence known in our bedroom, we both felt him enter and simultaneously we hit the floor and began to travail until the sun came up. By this time, the uneasiness of the presence of the warlock was gone, now we were tired of this nuisance. Needless to say, our bodies were also tired because we had not really slept in two days. The third night came, and as usual Marc and I were in the bed but this night we sat up, watched, and waited for him to show up as long as we could. But we got sleepy and dozed off.

Now this night the warlock got brave. As I drifted off to sleep the moment my eyes closed completely, I could feel three thick pointy fingernails slide down my back. My eyes popped opened, I turned around looked him in the face and shouted, "THIS IS YOUR LAST NIGHT!!!" Marc heard me and with no questions asked he jumped up and we both hit the floor because he knew what time it was. And we travailed, and travailed, and travailed until daybreak.

When morning came our youngest son, Zachariah who was five at the time, came in our room and sat between Marc and I on the bed. We were in conversation with Zach when we all heard something heavy on the roof of the house. It ran across the roof and leaped; we all heard its claws scraping the roof as it left.

Zach shouted, "DADDY WHAT WAS THAT?!" Marc and I looked at each other as if we were both thinking the exact same thing.
Then Marc asked, "Zach you heard that?"
Zach replied, "Yes, I heard that. What was that on the roof?"
Marc said, "Do not worry son it is gone."
Right at that moment I heard the Lord say, "The warlock is gone, he came to abort Marc's and your destiny that you are carrying, you are pregnant in the natural and in the spirit. You will give birth to both at the same time." Shortly after Anna was born Marc's ordination service as pastor happened.

Elevation in the spirit does not come without a fight but we never expected that we would literally have to fight in the natural for this type of elevation. There were many times that Marc and I would have to wrestle like this where beings from the demonic realm would come to us in the natural. I can remember when I wrestled in the natural with a demonic force, we came home from church and the dark force met me at the house. Marc, the children, and I had just finished eating dinner when out of the blue I was almost pinned down by a force and I felt the most excruciating pain I ever felt in my life. Remember I had given birth to five children. It was my feet; my feet were being moved by a force that was not me. This force was pulling back my toes and distorting them in a way that you would see on a movie. Except it was not a movie, it was real. All I could do was call out, "JESUS, JESUS HELP!!!" Marc and the children ran to me as I screamed in agony. When they got to me, they all gathered around and just stood there and watched in disbelief. They looked terrorized because they have never seen anything like this happen in real life before. Neither had I, I was just as spooked as they were.

Chris, our second eldest son shouted, "Daddy why Mama feet doing that, who's doing that to mama?!!" Thank God I have a praying husband, Marc told the children to hold hands and pray this spirit off mama. And as they all prayed the pain slowly eased off of my feet and my toes straightened back to normal. But the tears that streamed down my face did not stop because I could not understand why the Lord, whom I gave my life to, would allow this to happen to me.

Assuming that the Father heard my thoughts and was looking at the whole event unfold spoke to me and said, "I allowed this to happen, now when you come in contact with witchcraft you will immediately feel it in your feet. Whether it is designed for you or anyone else if it is near you, you will know and recognize it immediately." And then God explained deeper. "There were two demonic forces that day one was already at the house waiting for you and another one attached itself to something that someone, who did not like you, had given you when you left the restaurant." The next weeks turned into months of God teaching Marc and I the depths and many levels of witchcraft. That teaching will be in another book.

Global Impartation

September 11, 2011, I awoke out of a deep sleep seeing the whole continent of Africa. So, I asked the Lord, "Why am I seeing the continent of Africa?"
He simply replied, "They shall see me first when I crack the sky." In my mind I knew He was speaking on the Coming of Christ. And then very softly I heard, "I am opening a door for you to go." Being extremely sleepy I fell right back into a deep sleep. You never know just how God will fulfill His promises to you. Especially when you cannot see it coming to pass due to an obstructed view of your future.

Even as a child, I always knew that I would get to the continent of Africa someday, but just did not know when or how. After all, Mama did not name me after the great mother Yaa Asantewaa of the Ashanti tribe for nothing, I was going even if it was just for my name's sake. Africa is dear to the heart of God as well as the whole earth is near to His heart but there is something special about Africa. After learning how to battle in the spirit nationally it was time we learned how to battle globally. God began dealing with Marc and I about global ministry. We began researching what to do, as well as how to go about it. Several years later we attended a local global missions' school in Winston Salem, NC. The global Impartation happened there. In the midst of the program, we relocated back to Atlanta as instructed by the Lord. The global mandate remained heavily on our hearts but every opportunity that came we were not in a position to go, it was not time.

One day the door opened for me to go. Even with the open door, I still said I could not go because I did not have all of the money. But God! He stepped in and reminded me of the time He promised me that He would send me to Africa. I believed Him but still looked at the bank account saying, "I do not know how this *'gon* happen Lord."

But God! He made it so my plane ticket, vaccines, and visas were all paid for. So even if I tried to back out God would have said, "now what's your excuse?" Everything was paid in full! God had caused men to give unto my bosom. Luke 6:38 states, *Give, and it shall be given to you. A good measure, pressed down, shaken together, and running over, shall men give unto your bosom, for with the same measure that you measure, it shall be measured back to you again.* People at times do not know why they are helping you, nor do they realize that God is using them to fulfill a promise He made to you. Perhaps, God has not revealed to them who you really are in the spirit, so they will look at it as though they are helping you. When in fact, it is merely Gods favor upon you for them to act as His agents to complete a task already planned for your life. In turn, they too are blessed because they were there to assist God in fulfilling your destiny. So, on my way to Africa, I went with only $250, a plane ticket, visa all paid for and a bunch of faith in my pocket. Even though I paid them all of it back, I was grateful. When God says go there is no stopping you, He will pave the way for you without any strain.

Memoirs of a Girl Prophet

My first trip to Africa was an easy trip; not much warfare went on. However, my second trip, whew!! The warfare was extremely heavy, Marc and I had never seen nor experienced this type of spiritual warfare before. Marc, myself, and the Global World Missions prayer team all were getting hit hard with spiritual warfare. I mean HARD! So hard in fact that Marc, the kids, and I were literally homeless for two weeks during Christmas. We went from living in a beautiful 4300 sq ft. home to living in a hotel suite. It all happened so quick we thought we were dreaming. We could not believe it. Homeless Lord? Really Lord? Ok this is crazy we all thought. I have never been homeless before; you know you are homeless when you are expecting important mail to come but you do not have an address to send it too.

Thank God we had a little savings and a loving family that stepped in to help us financially. It was such a humbling and learning experience for sure. We kept repeating the scriptures, "I have never seen the righteous forsaken nor His seed begging bread." And "God shall supply all our needs according to His riches and glory." So, what did we do? We did what we knew to do, we went to the Lord. We would repeat those scriptures all day, every day until we walked into our new home. He told us with this level of warfare you must know your attacker by name. So, we asked Him who was it that was attacking us. And He began talking to us about the alligator spirit that came up out of the Atlantic Ocean to eat up our money, livelihood and not only did it hit us it hit the whole prayer team as well. **Know this, whatever hits the head affects the body.** This was different and not only were we battling the alligator spirit, but God revealed that jealousy, territorialism, and witchcraft stepped in too!

So, we had to learn and apply a different strategy for global warfare. God told us that the alligator spirit came from the marine spirit which was from overseas in the land where we were heading. The witch doctors heard of our coming to do the Lords' excellent work, so they assembled together and sent a missile attacking our finances to hinder us from coming. The jealousy and territorial spirit came from American people who did not really want us to administer global missions. The Lord kept warning us about this person negatively saying this or saying that, when they heard of our global assignment. Wow this was coming from the church, surprising is it not? The jealousy and territorial spirits were easy to tame but the marine spirit was our real fight. Once we were victorious over all the attacks God lead us to and through the continent of Africa effortlessly and back home and without harm. God also gave us favor on a new home and increased our bank account in that same year! God is a restorer; He will replenish all that is lost, if you just keep the faith. Our Heavenly Father has never once failed us, and He never will. God is good.

Chapter 6

Holy Spirit Sat On My Bed And Cried.

Insensitive is defined as being deprived of sensation; unconscious; unfeeling gifts and callings are without repentance.

Meaning that God has given all a measure of His spiritual and/or natural gifts. We know and understand that Holy Spirit administers God's gifts to His people. We also understand that without Holy Spirit, God cannot be revealed.

Holy Spirit stands back and waits to be introduced. Holy Spirit eagerly stands by waiting for us to introduce Him to those that do not know Him yet. And just imagine the sadness you feel when you are present in the room of friends, but you go unnoticed or looked over by everyone. He feels that a lot and I wonder if He ponders on the thought if He will get introduced or not. He is a gentleman, you see, so Holy Spirit will never intrude on you making it awkward. He desires His first meeting with you to be sweet and pleasant, peaceful, and welcome. He is such a gentleman in fact, that He does not announce Himself when He is in the room. He just quietly comes in and waits for you to acknowledge that He is present. It amazes me how insensitive the people of God can be when He is present. Anyway, how could they introduce Him to anyone if they are not even aware that He is in the room? He is everywhere and in everything, He is omnipresent, a mighty rushing wind is how He is described in the book of Acts.

> *And suddenly there came a sound from Heaven as of a mighty rushing wind and it filled the whole house where they were sitting. Acts 2:2*

For years I would refer to Holy Spirit as an it—not meaning any harm and certainly not meaning any disrespect. I can remember in 2003 I was talking to Holy Spirit, and I felt a slight agitation from Him, but I went on talking until He abruptly but calmly stopped me and said, "I wish you would not do that." Everything in me stopped, I immediately stopped talking so that I could hear what He had to say next. He continued, "I am a person, like you and I do not like it when people call me it." My mouth dropped opened and I just froze because that was the very first time that He spoke to me regarding how He felt about how I addressed Him during our daily talks. And He continued with, "When God the Father speaks to you, you address Him as such. When Jesus comes to you, you address Him as such but when you speak of me, you call me it. Learn to recognize which entity is in the room or which voice is speaking with you at the moment."

Remember when I said that I froze when Holy Spirit started speaking, well now my jaw was wide open, my eyes were huge, and I could not move. As

Holy Spirit left the room, I slowly sat down on the edge of my bed feeling sorry for unknowingly hurting the one that I loved. I only called Him it because that is what I heard the church call Him all of my life. And from that day on I was on a quest to learn the distinction between which presence of the Trinity it was that spoke to me. I now ask, "who is it that is speaking to me." And they always announce themselves when I am not sure who is present at the time. Always keep in mind that they are one but have different personalities.

When God the Father speaks you, you instantly know who it is that is speaking to you without question. Your spirit man automatically comes into alignment with the Father. Whether you believe in Him or not your spirit man knows who He is; even though I have only heard the Fathers' voice audibly twice in my life. Both times I immediately knew that it was the Father speaking. Not Jesus or Holy Spirit but Father Himself. His voice is deep, rich, and sounds as if it comes from a faraway place but yet is still nearby. It is heavy like coming from an extremely gigantic unearthly being. If I could compare it to anything it sounds like all the worlds natural elements are speaking. Earth, Water, Air, and fire, all mixed into His vocals. I felt loved hearing it as though from an earthly father as he would speak to his daughter. The love for me that I heard in His voice commanded me to quickly obey Him.

My sheep will know my voice and a stranger they will not follow. John 10: 4-5

Memoirs of a Girl Prophet

The 1st time I heard the Fathers' voice He spoke very sternly. And my spirit quickened with obedience. He was warning me of a potential hidden danger that I was in from the person that I was visiting. Even though I knew I did not need to be with the young man, it was curiosity that led me there. My curiosity led me to an unsafe place, God saw that and spoke, "Yaa go home." I acknowledged that I heard Him but did not move. A few seconds later I heard, "Yaa go HOME." Again, I acknowledged that it was the Father speaking to me, but I still did not move. And then I heard, "YAA GO HOME!!!!"

I jumped up and told the person to take me home. He did not move quickly enough so I shouted, "TAKE ME HOME NOW!!"

He turned and said, "ok come on let's go." But the look in his eyes was like, *what the world is wrong with this girl*. As a matter of fact, that same person somehow found out how precise my hearing from God was, and he offered me a position to work with him as a medium for money. That was the danger God saw. My prophetic gift was about to be misused. I learned that God the Father does not audibly use His voice to speak directly to His prophets often but when He does it is for something major that He needs **corrected**. God is continuously giving us signs of who He is.

When Jesus comes to you, He just shows up without warning like He did in Daniel 3. And we know and honor Him as the King of Glory as it states in Psalms 24:8. Jesus can make Himself known and unknown to men. He can change Himself and appear in diverse ways. When Yahshua appears to you He comes with great power and in my personal encounters with Him I always feel the warmth of a bright light from Him in the room or He will show me only the back of Himself, never His face. In which I asked Him one time, "why do you only show me the back of you?"

Jesus answered, "Yaa you are not ready to see my face yet." I do not press the issue whenever He allows me to see His face, I am sure it will be at the perfect time. Several times I have felt the healing power of Jesus on my body. I remember I injured my hip, and I would sometimes feel pain in it on my right side. The pain would cause me to limp a little when I walked. Funny thing is that nobody ever noticed it and I never said anything about it to anyone.

I went to church one day and the minister was preaching and then he stopped in mid thought and looked at me and said, "God is about to heal your right hip." And he went right back to preaching. But as soon as the minister finished saying that to me, I felt a soothing, warm feeling going down the right side of my body to the hip area. After that day I have never had that pain or limp again. I know Jesus as my healer and my deliverer. I cannot count the many times that He has come to my aid. As a matter of fact, every time I call on Him to heal me He does.

I asked God one time "why every time I called on Jesus to heal me, He comes? And why when I called on Him to heal my mother He did not, and she died?"

He answered, "I have work for you to do and I need your body." Such a simple answer to a perplexing question. Later I understood that my mom's death happened because she was ready to go, she was tired. Amazingly I have been healed so many times from things that should have killed me but did not because Yahshua always steps in. I cannot even begin to talk about all the healings and near-death experiences that took place in my life. We shall save that for another book.

Although we cannot fully understand God, we can still know Him through a personal relationship of faith and through studying His word. So now that you understand the different entities of the Trinity, I can explain to you what this chapter is about.

There are Thousands.
August 26, 2008

The Lord woke me up at 3:05 am—I have a habit of looking at the time when He awakes me. I sat up on my bed and I began praying asking God what is it that He needed from me. I did not hear Him answer and really did not think much of it. Still praying quietly because I did not want to wake Marc, I looked at the time again and it was then 4:10 am. I thought, He woke me up for something, but I am not hearing Him say anything. So, I got off the bed and got down on my knees beside the bed and continued to pray quietly. Anytime I get on my knees I am lowering and humbling myself to get in His presence. Sometimes I even lay prostrate for a deeper connection with Him. However, sometimes the power of God will lay me out prostrate and paralyzed from my neck down to my feet. That is a lesson in prayer that I will teach in another book.

On my knees still waiting to hear God say something. I only heard silence, I looked at the time again it was 5:01 am. And again, I heard nothing from Him. Sensing something was going on in the spirit I stopped praying got up off the floor and sat on the edge of my bed and softly asked, "What is it God?" As soon as I said that, I felt the bed go down as if someone was sitting next to me. I looked over to my left and my bed had an imprint on it as it would if someone was sitting there; only I could not visibly see Him. But I knew it was Holy Spirit.

And then I heard Him weeping intensely. Holy Spirit softly began to speak to me fighting His tears so I could understand Him. These were His words, "They do not know how much they grieve me." In my mind I thought that He was talking of local ministers that Marc and I knew were in error. Holy Spirit knowing my thoughts interrupted my thoughts with, "not one but thousands." Still weeping Holy Spirit continued, "my pastors and leaders in the kingdom are not sensitive to my feelings concerning obedience to me." Right then I began to quietly weep because I felt how deeply saddened He was. And began to wonder to myself, who am I that Holy Spirit will come to me and express His feelings with me? I am a nobody I thought and those around me do not even accept nor acknowledge the prophetic gifting in me. I heard Him continue to cry and so I did also. We sat on the side of my bed and wept for the nation together.

Chapter 7

A Consuming Fire

August 6, 2010

I dreamt that I was in the kitchen around noon. The children were out of school for summer break and playing somewhere in their rooms; Marc was at work. In the dream I was in the kitchen cleaning when I noticed a small fire outside on the deck. I ran outside to see where the fire was coming from because I was afraid that it would spread to burn down the house. I looked down and saw where the flames actually were coming from. The flames were spurting out of a small round metal container. So, I ran in the kitchen and filled a few pots of water. I ran back outside and began dumping the water on the fire, but the strangest thing was happening. The more I poured water on the flames they would not go out. I did this several times, but the flame kept burning. I also noticed that the trees were swaying with the wind, but the flames did not blow in the direction with the wind they just consistently burned upright.

So, I stood still and stared at this whole unbelievable situation, which went on for what seemed like a long time. I observed that the deck by now should be on fire, but it was not. I began to notice that that was no smell of fire. I was puzzled. I did not know what to do. So, I began to dump water on the flame again, and yet the flame did not go out.

So, I began to ask God what was the meaning of it? And He simply let me know that His presence dwelled with us at that house. We lived in the home in Winston Salem for fifteen years. So many blessings and visitations from Heaven happened in that home. Our ministry was birthed in that home, we had church services in the basement of that home. Marquis, our eldest son would see Angels walking back and forth by the fence in our yard on his way to the school bus stop. He also gave his life to the Lord in that home. God surly dwelled in that home.

Chapter 8

Vision of 9/11

September 2, 2001

An open vision came to me of a plane flying between two tall buildings above busy city streets. The vision came to me like a flash, it was so vivid and seemed so close that I could sense something major was coming. Marc happened to be sitting right next to me and I casually said, "Honey, we are going to be flying cars that look like small planes in the future." Not remembering what he said back to me but how wrong was I!

On September 11, 2001, I was watching the breaking news on tv because America was under a terrorist attack. While watching the news I saw the images of the same plane that I saw in my vision. That was when I realized that God was warning me that America was about to be under attack. At that time in my life, I did not know how to effectively use the prophetic gift God gave me to warn people of upcoming destruction. Nor did I have anyone to help guide me with this prophetic call on my life. I had to learn it through trial, error and with the help of Holy Spirit and my husband's knowledge of the word of God. Together we would match my supernatural experiences with the reading of the Bible to get a clearer understanding of what exactly was happening in my life. Which is another reason I am authoring this book, to help those who have a prophetic gift but do not have the guidance to walk in it productively.

About two weeks after the attacks the voice of the Lord came to me and said, "Yaa pray for the people that are trapped under the rubble of the buildings, pray that they are found." And He began giving me the names of some of the people that were still alive but injured sitting in pockets of openings under the rubble waiting and praying to be rescued. In about a week later after continuously praying the news reported people were beginning to be lifted out from the rubble. And my heart was glad because even though no one knew that God called out the names in secret to Marc and myself to be rescued. One by one we rejoiced with tears in our eyes when we watched the news of them being brought out from beneath what should have killed them.

Although many people lost their lives on that dreadful day God showed up, instead of sending the angels to report back to Him what was happening. God Himself showed up to look in on the matter. God had us to intercede for their lives and even though we may never meet them our hearts are glad that they made it out to safety. God called them out by name what an honor to be called out by the Master Himself of a terrible mishap. Amen!

Weeks later I was sitting still as I normally do when God is about to rest His Spirit upon me. But this time it was not so pleasant, I began hearing cries and yells from terror or torture. And all of a sudden, I smelled this awful smell. Then I heard the Lord say to me, "Yaa some did not make it, you are hearing their cries from Hell and the smell that you smell is sulfur, a stench that remains there." I began to weep for them.

People, please understand that Hell is a real place in eternity. God loves us so much that He sends ordinary people like you and me to warn others of such a place. And what you do or how you live your life here on earth determines where you will spend your eternal life. After the planes crashed into the Twin Towers in New York I saw a vision of the aftermath of the city. God allowed me to see the imprint of His transparent face pressed against the open sky. The shape of His face looked that of a male face. The size of His face was so enormous that stretched across a substantial portion of the sky. It is very unusual for Him to show Himself in that manner because I know that God likes to hide Himself.

> *Truly you are a God who hides Himself, O God of Israel, Savior!" Isaiah 45:15*
> *"You shall seek me and find me when you search for me with all your heart. And I will be found of you saith the Lord.*
> *Jeremiah 29:13-14*

There are over thirty scriptures in the Bible that explains why He hides Himself. But because America, a country that He loves, was under attack He made His presence known to us. We needed to see Him during that dark time in America. As I looked closely at Him, He was looking down watching all of the trauma and devastation that took place on America's soil that day. It was a land that honored Him greatly and many of His appointed servants are in America, so it caught His immediate attention. It took that horrible event that allowed so many of His saints to simultaneously see Him in different ways. Just to let America know that He is still with us. We had Bible study on Wednesdays and after one Bible study I mustered up enough courage to share with my church members what God had shown me in the vision.

And to my surprise my fellow church member, Evangelist Peggy Wagner, walked over to me pulling a piece of paper out from her bible. And she said to me, "Is this what you saw?" She showed me a copy of a picture that someone had drawn of the exact same vision that I saw. God had shown many people His face pressed against the sky because He knew we needed to see Him in a major way and that we need not worry because He is with us. That was the confirmation I needed at the time. Because during those days I was still learning how to interpret the things that God was showing me in secret.

> *"For where two or three are gathered together in my name, there I am in the midst of them." Matthew 18:20*

Chapter 9

Arms of Vines Dream

November 2000

In the early years of my marriage, I would often think about what if my marriage ended up like my mother's, in divorce. I was afraid of that happening so much that it was always on my heart, forbidding me to fully commit in relationships. After marrying Marc, one night I was in a deep sleep and all of a sudden, my forearms began to itch really badly. Before I realized it, I was dreaming. In the dream my arms itched so badly that I started to scratch furiously and whelps from my nails began to form. While scratching, I looked down at my arms and they began to turn from my brown skin to an odd yellowish color but were growing at the same time. I was startled to watch them turn from brown to yellow and from yellow to green. They turned into long green vines that extended from my elbows.

Could you imagine how terrified and confused I was because I did not understand what was happening. I looked over to my right side and saw a machete knife laying on the floor. I picked up the knife and cut the two vines that extended from my elbows that had grown about 12 feet from my arms. I watched the two cut vines die as they turned dry and brittle. By this time, they had grown into these long thick green vines that kind of reminded me of kudzu vines because they had leaves on them.

After cutting the vines I saw that my arms and hands were back to normal, I began to feel normal again until I heard the voice of God say to me almost in a shout as though I angered Him, "Yaa if you cut me off, I will cut you off!" and immediately with great speed, the vines grew back longer and much thicker and greener than the vines before. But something even more strange began to happen, the two vines begin to intertwine as one and grew up into a large tree trunk and continued to grow up in the air then I saw branches began to sprout from the trunk of the tree. This tree had large green leaves on them from its branches. From the vines grew a full mature tree. I looked again and saw that it was I that became the tree itself which was planted by what looked like a white mansion with large kingdom like columns. And planted right beside me was another taller and fuller tree, more mature than I, which was a representation of Marc, my husband. Then three other smaller trees with names on them appeared and those were my children. And at the time I had this dream only Marquis, Chris, and Indya were born. Zach and Anna were not born at that time. And we all swayed with the wind planted firmly in a safe and nurturing place in peace.

Two weeks later Marc came to me and warmly said, "Honey, I found your dream in the scriptures." Then he opened the Bible to John 15.

"1 I am the true vine, and my Father is the gardener. 2 He cuts off every branch in me that bears no fruit, while every branch that does bear fruit he prunes[a] so that it will be even more fruitful. 3 You are already clean because of the word I have spoken to you. 4 Remain in me, as I also remain in you. No branch can bear fruit by itself; it must remain in the vine. Neither can you bear fruit unless you remain in me. 5 "I am the vine; you are the branches. If you remain in me and I in you, you will bear much fruit; apart from me you can do nothing. 6 If you do not remain in me, you are like a branch that is thrown away and withers; such branches are picked up, thrown into the fire and burned. 7 If you remain in me and my words remain in you, ask whatever you wish, and it will be done for you. 8 This is to my Father's glory, that you bear much fruit, showing yourselves to be my disciples. 9 "As the Father has loved me, so have I loved you. Now remain in my love. 10 If you keep my commands, you will remain in my love, just as I have kept my Father's commands and remain in his love. 11 I have told you this so that my joy may be in you and that your joy may be complete. 12 My command is this: Love each other as I have loved you. 13 Greater love has no one than this: to lay down one's life for one's friends. 14 You are my friends if you do what I command. 15 I no longer call you servants, because a servant does not know his master's business. Instead, I have called you friends,

for everything that I learned from my Father I have made known to you. 16 You did not choose me, but I chose you and appointed you so that you might go and bear fruit—fruit that will last—and so that whatever you ask in my name the Father will give you. 17 This is my command: Love each other. John 15

After reading and meditating on this scripture the spirit of "what if this happens" left me. And I became confident in what the Lord had given me, a Godly family. God the Father will give you dreams, visions, or similitudes of His word before you even read them. Remember it was only by Gods Divine inspiration that Moses wrote the first five books of the Bible. And knowing there is such a great Divine Being amongst us, which is God the Father, as for me and my house we will serve the Lord.

Chapter 10

Thorn in my Flesh

I have often wondered why Apostle Paul mentioned in the book of 2 Corinthians that he had a thorn in his flesh. I thought that he had a thorn injected somewhere on his body that brought him great pain for serving the Lord. There are so many conspiracies that explains Paul's thorn but how would they really know. It was not until I myself began to have awful pains that would come on my body out of nowhere. They would hurt so bad that I would go to the hospital and the doctors would do X-rays, examine me from head to toe but would find nothing wrong with me. I remember one doctor, after he did everything he knew to do, looked at me long, hard, and said, "Ma'am I can see that you are in a lot of pain but there is nothing medically wrong with you." Marc and I looked at him like he clearly did not want to help me. But honestly speaking every doctor would give the same conclusion. Nothing was wrong with me. But it was! I was in pain, an unexplainable pain and no one could help me. I began questioning God about this pain that would come unexpectedly. He finally answered but with pain.

One day coming out of Bible study I felt a slight pain in my right ankle. My Overseer Lois Hargrave, which was my husband's grandmother, saw me limping and said, "Yaa what did you do to your ankle?"

I answered her, "Overseer I do not know my ankle just started hurting out the blue." I asked her to pray for it as we left church. So, when Marc the children and I got home I put some rubbing alcohol on it thinking that would help. It did not; unbelievably the pain began to increase a little. I did not think much of it until I heard these words, "Yaa this pain you feel in your ankle will happen for three days." And that was it, that was all I heard God say. But what he did not tell me was that the pain would increase each day. The next morning my ankle was still hurting but a little more. I was still able to hop around the house getting the kids ready for school, cook, clean and other chores. It was doable and tolerable.

However, later that night the pain hit like someone was turning a dagger in my right ankle. After childbirth, my tolerance of pain was pretty high. This pain in my ankle was so much greater than birth pains. The pain literally would take my breath away at times. All Marc could do was try to console me and rub my ankle, but the pain was so great at times I could not stand for anything to touch it. I thought, what did I do so bad that God would allow me to suffer at this magnitude? I began screaming crying asking God in my agony, "What did I do!?!" I heard nothing.

The next day came which was the third day. On this day I was in so much pain that I stretched out across the bed and just screamed and cried. But I noticed something the same light and warmth that was in my room as a child was present with me as the pain increased. Holy Spirit was present watching in the room. Hopelessly Marc and the children would silently watch me in agony wanting to help but could not. It was between me and God.

Later into the night the pain increased again, it was so unbearable that God finally had mercy on me and spoke these words, "Yaa I allowed this pain on you because of where I am taking you, you have to remain humble. I will not allow you to walk in arrogance. When you wake up tomorrow the pain will be gone." Crying hysterically and in the most pain I ever physically felt in my life, I somehow felt comforted. Only because my Father spoke to me and gave me His reason for this intrusion on my body. I told Marc what God had said and cried myself to sleep in Marc's arms. Marc's love for me helped me through the pain.

When I woke up the next day I wriggled my ankle, and the pain was completely gone! Everything happened exactly how God instructed it would. Although joyful and relieved the pain was gone, I began to wonder why would I become arrogant? I do not even like arrogant people so why would I become that which I hated? My thoughts began racing all over the place. And then I realized how many ministers arrogantly pride themselves of their accomplishments in the name of the Lord. And how arrogantly some ministers look down upon so many people, Gods people. I thought I do not ever want to become like that. So, God began showing me ministers that operate from an arrogant spirit, He trained my eye to recognize it immediately. And I began to notice the ministers He would tell Marc and I to intercede for praying for their deliverance from the arrogant spirit. And I also noticed the ones He does not tell us to intercede for as well.

There are many ministers today gracing pulpits locally, nationally, and internationally with the same arrogant spirit that God trained my eye to spot which got Lucifer thrown from heaven. Sadly, most of them will ever heed to submitting themselves under true spiritual authority to receive rebuke and deliverance. They have become accustomed to being treated as "rock stars" in the body of Christ. That is dangerous ground because they are the ones that truly do not understand real spiritual authority. Spiritual authority does not come from one who has been in ministry the longest, has the biggest name, has the most engagements, or with the most accomplishments or accolades. It is quiet Ananias from Damascus who was a disciple of Jesus who was sent to restore sight to Paul, who Paul studied under for fourteen years before Paul ever wrote out his first sermon. Ananias's name may not be as great as Paul's in the earth, but he carried a great amount of Spiritual Authority to push Paul into the great Apostle that he became.

It is the humbleness of a minister that receives the most weight with God. To walk in true spiritual authority is not loud and boastful among men but gentle enough that a whisper can move mountains in someone's life without them even knowing. And then being meek enough to never boast about it. Through my own personal journey with God, I have realized at times people will equate your level of anointing to your public accomplishments. I beg to differ; your level of anointing comes from how long you stay in the presence of God; building an intimate relationship with him. That and only that will determine the amount of weight you carry in God.

I do not feel that intense pain often but when I do I know that it is Gods gentle reminder for me not go down the road that many have before me. Over the years as the pain reaches its peak on the third day each one of my children have asked me why God allows this on me. I make certain to tell them why, knowing that they still really do not understand. But I appreciate my children's patience with me as they carry me to my bed because the pain is too great for me to walk. We have been quietly doing this now for over fifteen years. My children know and understand who God is according to how He deals with Marc and myself at home. And through it all without question they love Him too, that pleases me.

Chapter 11

Vision of the Lake of Fire

Being that prophetic dreams, visions, or similitudes come to me regularly, I have become accustomed to being interrupted by God's presence suddenly. Thankfully, my husband and children are too. I remember walking in the hallway. The moment I sat down on my bed I was in another dimension, where I was running wildly. I looked to my right and there were hundreds of thousands of gray souls in the form of men. I am running at the forefront of them, unaware as to why. Then I saw myself yelling, screaming, and waving my hands at them motioning them to go back. But they were not paying attention; so, I ran harder and faster yelling with all my might, "GO BACK, GO BACK, GO BACK!!!!" Tirelessly it seemed I ran for miles until I looked over to my left and saw that we were close to a cliff, I ran closer to the cliff so I could see what was below. While running at full speed I looked down the cliff and saw a boiling red lava lake.

The gray souls were blindly walking in rhythm, as though someone had commanded them to go forward and not stop. I noticed that I was running between them and the boiling lava lake, but they did not heed my warning. I quickly turned around and saw one of the souls fall into the lava lake. Then immediately the vision was gone and I began weeping. I asked God what happened. Because I knew that those souls were assigned to me, and one fell in. That grieved me. In that moment I made a firm decision not to lose any souls assigned to me by God.

People of God, listen to me. Each of us have a number of souls assigned to our life. We the body of Christ, are responsible for these souls to make it into heaven and inherit eternal life. And what we do in our life affects the destiny of someone else's life. It is imperative that you understand that you are not just here on earth for yourself. This is God the Father's story; He is the Potter, and we are the clay. However, He desires to mold us is for our betterment. It is wise not to resist His plan for our lives. Even though God gave us the right to choose, He will never overstep your will. He made us in His image remember, having the ability to use our own thoughts just as He does. The angels are limited in their own thinking abilities which is why they look at humans puzzled. Because they see how God deals and cherishes the human race.

If you are reading this book and know that you have a call on your life, do not keep putting it off as I did. I urge you to quickly submit your life unto the Lord and do not let him wait on you any longer. He has a work for you to do, He is waiting on you. Answer Him. Do not be slow to answer Him like I did. Because in this vision one soul fell in the lava lake and I cannot help but wonder did I answer my call too late? Did my slothfulness to answer the call cause someone not reach their appointed destiny?

Chapter 12

The Coming of the Lord Dream

This chapter is most important one to me because it describes my true purpose for being on earth. In 2003, I had a dream my family and I were in a normal church service. Suddenly people began to get up and leave. As we left the building it was dark outside, so we hurried and got in the car. We drove down the street into a crowd of about fifteen to twenty unrecognizable people, standing in the middle of the street. They began surrounding our car and immediately Marc and I recognized that they were demonic. Marc drove faster to avoid this confrontation but as I looked around, I saw no other cars on the road. So, Marc pulled into an empty parking lot which had a fence with a large wrought iron gate around it.

I looked around and noticed that we were actually alone inside this massive parking lot. Desperately wanting to get out, I saw an escape, showed Marc and he sped through a hole in the gate. We drove around the corner and parked the car. We got and began walking not really knowing where we were going. And suddenly thousands of people appeared who were all trying to escape these same demonic beings that were trying to surround us again. While escaping these beings, I saw an extremely tall eight-foot individual. This man was wearing an eggplant-colored robe and hat but with all the commotion I did not pay him much attention; however, our paths would cross again as my family, and I were now making our way into a church. Still attempting to escape these demonic beings we were standing in a lengthy line desperately trying to enter.

Finally, inside of the church we saw men in the form of women and women in form of men. Marc and I both understood that this was **not** a Church of God. I turned around and saw the same eight-foot-tall individual inside of the church. And he turned and asked us, "Would you do something like that?" Without thinking Marc and I shouted, "Get away from me Satan!" We continued to shout, "I plead the blood of Jesus!"—over and over again! As we repeated those words this individual backed out of the church and into the street. We followed back outside of the church, amongst the thousands of people walking in the streets because it looked like a power outage had happened. The people heard Marc and I shouting, "I plead the BLOOD of Jesus!" Then the massive crowd began shouting, "Jesus! Jesus! Jesus! Jesus!" Collectively in one thunderous voice, pushing back the forces of evil. Then the tall demonic individual completely vanished!

I looked over to my left and saw animals of every kind begin lining up in perfect rows. But I noticed something odd happening, all of the animals began to bow down on one knee simultaneously. Then the people began singing, "People get ready, Jesus is coming soon we will be going home!" The sound of the multitude of people singing on one accord went all over the city. I looked around for my children and they were still standing by the church. I briefly turned my head and looked at Marc and then looked back at my children and to my surprise they were gone! A woman who helped us push back the demonic being saw me looking for my children. So, she pointed towards to the sky and shouted, "THEY WENT UP! THEY WENT UP!" So, Marc and I lined up alongside the multitude of people of all races and ethnicities. Simultaneously we all knelt down, looked up and saw the sky opening. A blinding light began to appear. Then I was immediately awakened when I heard God say this to me firmly, "Tell my people that Jesus is coming quickly!"

I was stunned. I sat up on my bed, tears began to softly run down my face. I realized the reason I was born; why God keeps me near Him even when I try to run away from Him. I am somehow quickly reeled back to Him without any effort on my part. My mind went back to when I was four years old, and a car almost hit me in downtown Atlanta; miraculously, an angel stepped in, and I escaped death. It was then I remembered when I was fifteen years old, being faced with a young man pointing a gun at me. Even though he glared into my eyes with anger, he could not pull the trigger because an Angel stepped in, and I walked away. That was actually my second face to face gun experience. I also remembered when I got older, I slept with someone not knowing that he was HIV positive. But he knew and had already passed it to other young ladies, but God blocked it from forming in me and I never contracted the disease. At that moment all the near death or traumatic experiences in my life came rushing into my mind. And then I heard God say, *"This is the reason why you were born, to tell people that my son is coming back for them."*

Now I understood why the grace and mercy of God the Father was with me, following me. Because I have a purpose here on earth. And so do you. It is up to you to discover what that purpose is.

People of God, Jesus is coming, and we must be ready. This dispensation that we call the church age is about to end. We, Gods Ecclesia, must remain steadfast and unshakable. Satan will try to tempt you all the way up until the return of Christ. So, it is imperative that you stay rooted and grounded in the word of God. Develop a deep and sincere relationship with our Father and you can only do that by getting in His presence daily. Do not get caught up in the new age that is happening around us in the world today but stand steadfast in the faith. Satan is clever and likes to use people of enormous influence or have the power to change laws and policies of the land to try and trip us up or take our focus off of our creator. Do not focus on the distractions but keep your eyes on Him that is able to keep us from falling. Because it is only by faith that we please Him. And it is by faith that we will make it into His kingdom. Amen.

> *Now unto him that is able to keep you from falling, and to present you faultless before the presence of his glory with exceeding joy, to the only wise God our Savior, be glory and majesty, dominion, and power, both now and ever. Amen. Jude 1:24-25*

INFORMATION

Yaa Carson is a speaker, prophetess, philanthropist, and now author. She and her husband, Marc, are founders of Global World Ministries based in Atlanta, Ga. Together they head mission teams from various parts of America going to underserved countries, spreading the good news of Jesus Christ. GWM focuses on bringing aid, empowering people, and equipping young entrepreneurs to build sustainability and take lead over poverty in their country. Yaa is the owner of Queen Yabee, Inc.

Operating in the office of a prophet, Yaa lives a life of total submission unto the Holy Spirit, and for many years being hidden under the protection of God, Yaa has learned the secret in being submissive under God's leading, understanding the importance of hearing and quickly obeying kingdom assignments given by the Father. Yaa is fervent about using her prophetic gift in delivering the Father's messages in clarity to His people. She and Marc are blessed with three sons, two daughters and two grandchildren.

For information for workshops, conference, lectures, and seminars please contact:

Yaa Carson
globalworldministries@yahoo.com

WWW.
GlobalWorldMinistries.org

www.ingramcontent.com/pod-product-compliance
Lightning Source LLC
Chambersburg PA
CBHW041131110526
44592CB00020B/2767